EMPLUMADA

Emplumada

Lorna Dee Cervantes

UNIVERSITY OF PITTSBURGH PRESS

Published by the University of Pittsburgh Press, Pittsburgh, Pa. 15260
Copyright © 1981, Lorna Dee Cervantes
Feffer and Simons, Inc., London
Manufactured in the United States of America

Library of Congress Cataloging in Publication Data

Cervantes, Lorna Dee.
  Emplumada.

  (Pitt poetry series)
  I. Title. II. Series.
PS3553.E79E47   811'.54   80-54063
ISBN 0-8229-3436-1   AACR2
ISBN 0-8229-5327-7 (pbk.)

Acknowledgment is made to the following periodicals for permission to re-
print some of the poems that appear in this book: *Beyond Rice, Canto Al
Pueblo, Contact II, Mango, Shankpainter, Tin Tan,* and *White Pine Journal.*

"Beneath the Shadow of the Freeway" and "Freeway 280" were originally
printed in *The Latin American Literary Review,* vol. 5, no. 10, 1977. The
following poems are reprinted with permission of *Revista Chicano-Riqueña*:
"Refugee Ship," from Año III, Num. 1, "Oaxaca, 1974," which originally
appeared under the title "Heritage" in Año IV, Num. 4, and "Como lo Siento,"
"The Body as Braille," and "Shells," which appeared in Año VI, Num. 3.

The author would like to extend a special thank-you to the Fine Arts Work
Center in Provincetown for a fellowship that allowed her to write many of
the poems included in this book, to the National Endowment for the Arts,
and to London Meadow for their support during the years 1972–1977.

*The publication of this book is supported by grants
from the National Endowment for the Arts
in Washington, D.C., a Federal agency,
and the Pennsylvania Council on the Arts.*

for John

em · plu · ma · do   *v.m.*, feathered; in plumage, as in after molting

plu · ma · da   *n.f.*, pen flourish

CONTENTS

CONTENTS

i

Consider the power of wrestling
your ally. His will is to kill you.
He has nothing against you.

UNCLE'S FIRST RABBIT

He was a good boy
making his way through
the Santa Barbara pines,
sighting the blast of fluff
as he leveled the rifle,
and the terrible singing began.
He was ten years old,
hunting my grandpa's supper.
He had dreamed of running,
shouldering the rifle to town,
selling it, and taking the next
train out.
                    Fifty years
have passed and he still hears
that rabbit "just like a baby."
He remembers how the rabbit
stopped keening under the butt
of his rifle, how he brought
it home with tears streaming
down his blood soaked jacket.
"That bastard. That bastard."
He cried all night and the week
after, remembering that voice
like his dead baby sister's,
remembering his father's drunken
kicking that had pushed her
into birth. She had a voice
like that, growing faint
at its end; his mother rocking,
softly, keening. He dreamed
of running, running
the bastard out of his life.

He would forget them, run down
the hill, leave his mother's
silent waters, and the sounds
of beating night after night.
                    When war came,
he took the man's vow. He was
finally leaving and taking
the bastard's last bloodline
with him. At war's end, he could
still hear her, her soft
body stiffening under water
like a shark's. The color
of the water, darkening, soaking,
as he clung to what was left
of a ship's gun. Ten long hours
off the coast of Okinawa, he sang
so he wouldn't hear them.
He pounded their voices out
of his head, and awakened
to find himself slugging the bloodied
face of his wife.
                    Fifty years
have passed and he has not run
the way he dreamed. The Paradise
pines shadow the bleak hills
to his home. His hunting hounds,
dead now. His father, long dead.
His wife, dying, hacking in the bed
she has not let him enter for the last
thirty years. He stands looking,
he mouths the words, "Die you bitch.

I'll live to watch you die." He turns,
entering their moss-soft livingroom.
He watches out the picture window
and remembers running: how he'll
take the new pickup to town, sell it,
and get the next train out.

CANNERY TOWN IN AUGUST

All night it humps the air.
Speechless, the steam rises
from the cannery columns. I hear
the night bird rave about work
or lunch, or sing the swing shift
home. I listen, while bodyless
uniforms and spinach specked shoes
drift in monochrome down the dark
moon-possessed streets. Women
who smell of whiskey and tomatoes,
peach fuzz reddening their lips and eyes—
I imagine them not speaking, dumbed
by the can's clamor and drop
to the trucks that wait, grunting
in their headlights below.
They spotlight those who walk
like a dream, with no one
waiting in the shadows
to palm them back to living.

THE ANTHILL

My palm cupped her mouth
As I kissed her, the flesh
Of my hand between us.
After school, we'd cross
The fields of wild mustard
To the anthills, to the Queen
Hiding in the dank recesses.
After school, my friend's throat
Ringed with daisies, so pale
And like me; I couldn't stand it—
All those bodies, moving.
An army of soldiers who had it
In for me. I could taste
Our salt. They could smell it,
Thousands of them, defending
Their missals as we kicked in
The nests to find her, and recover
The soft white packets
Of her young.

The Ally

He told her
shut up and die.
The bed of shrubs
in the vacant lot
listened and filled
the fog with their
"Tsk, tsk."
She was so young,
only two years
more than a child.
She felt the flex
of his arm before
he touched her,
the wind of his fist
before he hit her.
But it was the glint
of steel at her throat
that cut through
to her voice.
She would not be
silent and still.
She would live,
arrogantly,
having wrestled
her death
and won.

LOTS: II

Herself

I picked myself up   ignoring
whoever I was   slowly
noticing for the first time my body's stench
I made a list in my head
of all the names who could help me
and then   meticulously   I scratched
each one

>   *they won't hear me burning*
>   *inside of myself*

my used skin glistened
my first diamond

MEETING MESCALITO
AT OAK HILL CEMETERY

Sixteen years old and crooked
with drug, time warped blissfully
as I sat alone on Oak Hill.

The cemetery stones were neither erect
nor stonelike, but looked soft and harmless;
thousands of them rippling the meadows
like overgrown daisies.

I picked apricots from the trees below
where the great peacocks roosted and nagged
loose the feathers from their tails.
I knelt to a lizard with my hands
on the earth, lifted him and held him
in my palm—Mescalito
was a true god.

Coming home that evening
nothing had changed. I covered Mama on the sofa

with a quilt I sewed myself, locked my bedroom
door against the stepfather, and gathered
the feathers I'd found that morning, each
green eye in a heaven of blue, a fistfull
of understanding;

and late that night I tasted
the last of the sweet fruit, sucked the rich pit
and thought nothing of death.

BENEATH THE SHADOW
OF THE FREEWAY

1

Across the street—the freeway,
blind worm, wrapping the valley up
from Los Altos to Sal Si Puedes.
I watched it from my porch
unwinding. Every day at dusk
as Grandma watered geraniums
the shadow of the freeway lengthened.

2

We were a woman family:
Grandma, our innocent Queen;
Mama, the Swift Knight, Fearless Warrior.
Mama wanted to be Princess instead.
I know that. Even now she dreams of taffeta
and foot-high tiaras.

Myself: I could never decide.
So I turned to books, those staunch, upright men.
I became Scribe: Translator of Foreign Mail,
interpreting letters from the government, notices
of dissolved marriages and Welfare stipulations.
I paid the bills, did light man-work, fixed faucets,
insured everything
against all leaks.

3

Before rain I notice seagulls.
They walk in flocks,
cautious across lawns: splayed toes,
indecisive beaks. Grandma says
seagulls mean storm.

In California in the summer,
mockingbirds sing all night.
Grandma says they are singing for their nesting wives.
"They don't leave their families
borrachando."

She likes the ways of birds,
respects how they show themselves
for toast and a whistle.

She believes in myths and birds.
She trusts only what she builds
with her own hands.

4

She built her house,
cocky, disheveled carpentry,
after living twenty-five years
with a man who tried to kill her.

Grandma, from the hills of Santa Barbara,
I would open my eyes to see her stir mush
in the morning, her hair in loose braids,
tucked close around her head
with a yellow scarf.

Mama said, "It's her own fault,
getting screwed by a man for that long.
Sure as shit wasn't hard."
soft she was soft

5

in the night I would hear it
glass bottles shattering the street
words cracked into shrill screams
inside my throat   a cold fear
as it entered the house in hard
unsteady steps   stopping at my door
my name   bathrobe   slippers
outside a 3 A.M. mist heavy
as a breath full of whiskey
stop it   go home   come inside
mama if he comes here again
I'll call the police

inside
a gray kitten   a touchstone
purring beneath the quilts
grandma stitched
from his suits
the patchwork singing
of mockingbirds

6

"You're too soft . . . always were.
You'll get nothing but shit.
Baby, don't count on nobody."

—a mother's wisdom.
Soft. I haven't changed,
maybe grown more silent, cynical
on the outside.

"O Mama, with what's inside of me
I could wash that all away. I could."

"But Mama, if you're good to them
they'll be good to you back."

Back. The freeway is across the street.
It's summer now. Every night I sleep with a gentle man
to the hymn of mockingbirds,

and in time, I plant geraniums.
I tie up my hair into loose braids,
and trust only what I have built
with my own hands.

FOR EDWARD LONG

There are some who are not of this world.
Take what you need. Covet.
The child is one. They will comfort her soon.
E. L. (In a letter to my mother
from the Atascadero State Hospital.
Fall, 1965)

Pardner, you called me
that first morning my grandmother
found you, drunk, homeless, and you stayed
long enough to give me my voice.

You taught me to read all those windsongs
in the verses of Stevenson.
You'd pay me a quarter to sing on your lap
beneath the dust storm of your scruffy chin.
In those still nights your wine breath
sweetened the air for me.

You were father, grandfather, the man
who dug ditches for the county
and knew a code so secret
they locked it away.

Pardner, Doctor, crazy
mathematician and sometimes
wizard to the child I still am,
I still believe you.
I still gaze at the fall winds
you once taught me to describe.
I still shadow you. I know
wherever you are
you'll be reading poems
and this is how
I'll find you.

FOR VIRGINIA CHAVEZ

It was never in the planning,
in the life we thought
we'd live together, two fast
women living cheek to cheek,
still tasting the dog's
breath of boys in our testy
new awakening.
We were never the way
they had it planned.
Their wordless tongues we stole
and tasted the power
that comes of that.
We were never what they wanted
but we were bold. We could take
something of life and not
give it back. We could utter
the rules, mark the lines
and cross them ourselves—we two
women using our fists, we thought,
our wits, our tunnels. They were such
dumb hunks of warm fish
swimming inside us,
but this was love,
we knew, love, and that was all
we were ever offered.

You were always alone
so *another lonely life*
wouldn't matter.
In the still house
your mother left you,
when the men were gone
and the television droned
into test patterns, with our cups
of your mother's whiskey
balanced between the brown thighs
creeping out of our shorts, I read
you the poems of Lord Byron, Donne,
the Brownings: all about love,
explaining the words
before realizing that you knew
all that the kicks in your belly
had to teach you. You were proud
of the woman blooming out of your
fourteen lonely years, but you cried
when you read that poem I wrote you,
something about our "waning moons"
and the child in me
I let die that summer.

In the years that separate,
in the tongues that divide
and conquer, in the love
that was a language
in itself, you never spoke,
never regret. Even
that last morning
I saw you with blood
in your eyes, blood
on your mouth, the blood
pushing out of you
in purple blossoms.

He did this.
When I woke, the kids
were gone. They told me
I'd never get them back.

With our arms holding
each other's waists, we walked
the waking streets
back to your empty flat,
ignoring the horns and catcalls
behind us, ignoring what
the years had brought between us:
my diploma and the bare bulb
that always lit your bookless room.

CROW

She started and shot from the pine,
then brilliantly settled in the west field
and sunned herself purple.

I saw myself: twig and rasp, dry
in breath and ammonia smelling.
Women taught me to clean

and then build my own house.
Before men came they whispered,
Know good polished oak.

Learn hammer and Phillips.
Learn socket and rivet. I ran
over rocks and gravel they placed

by hand, leaving burly arguments
to fester the bedrooms. With my best jeans,
a twenty and a shepherd pup, I ran

flushed and shadowed by no one
alone   I settled   stiff in mouth
with the words women gave me.

COMMUNICATION

Are those beetles buzzing the lines
up there or is it the invention
of electricity? Maybe a daughter
is speaking to her mother long distance.
It's the lines of her parachute humming
as she plunges out of her chosen element.
The fall back to her mother
is a castle's dance straight down
through air like the drop
from a 747 over the desert flower
of cat-colored gorges;
it's check, and mate.

"Mama, it's me, finally."

And finally, it is me
only guessing at what secrets
or hatreds they share.
As I pass the streets of another
unexplored city, I hear in the wires
that first tentative, *Hello?*
It hangs over my head, as alive
as electricity, or a beetle's eloquent
wing, aloft, or a foot, rowing,
as she pedals her bicycle away.

CARIBOU GIRL

I loved Caribou Girl,
for the woman she promised
to become, for the crows
who spoke and sent her poems,
sent her sleek black love letters.
All she ever had to do was skip-jump,
whistle, master the art
of her dance: a certain arch of back,
method of spin. She knew
she could dance.

I loved the girl some thought too strange,
too dark, who spoke the cadence
of her own mythology, her own sanity,
with the words from books
trailing her lips like shadows.
She wants to give them to the world
con un abrazo.
She wants to speak them like her father
who lives them.

He is Great Brown. He is Too High.
She mews on the ground
before him like a little
cat.

Wankan Tanka is nothing
but the mockingbird
who sings to his mate at midnight,
nothing but the crows who play
in the schoolyard, nothing
but the birds who leave me
gifts of feathers.

I dream four great hawks and a speckled bird.
I dream Quetzalcoátl, Ometeótl, the Great Manitou
who leaves me a vision to make me strong,
who lifts me to birds
from a mere
cat girl.

I have learned the serenity
of a mockingbird, the justice
of a crow, blue jay's strength;
I've dipped their feathers in blood
to seal the pact—my path.

The girl some thought too strange
found books that echoed her dream,
found a man who dreamt as she,
and she sent father kisses
on the backs of her crows
and she prayed he wouldn't go
crazy.

I loved her, loved
the little tricks of the sane,
loved the balance of hooves
and the wade through ice.

In the distance I see her slip from the rocks,
see her once more try to walk on water.
I know she can't fly.
I've seen her trade feathers
for those hooves, for that sleek tan skin.
She slips from the rocks,
a thin crazed girl,
who wore blue-jay feathers and moccasins,
and to whom everything was sacred.
She slips from the rocks
and I know she will drown.

I answer her: the wet
clothes are between my fingers,
a curling smoke of cold hair
trails my ankles, but I'm going
to leave her
for another breath
before I plunge
with her again.

This world understands nothing but words
and you have come into it with almost none.
—Antonio Porchia

THE PRAYER PRESSED
BETWEEN THE WAVES

There's sky and death
shimmering the waves.
He may never come back.
He may be forced to enter
the dumbness of tides,
he may swim, locked
in the freezing minutes
left him. But think
of her, mooning from her
widow's roost, stunned while
sighting the horizon's disarray.
She may hear the foreign tongue
the gulls speak, meddling, or
she may notice the silvery tern
buckle and dive, reentering
with something flashing in its beak.
And afterwards, she may never see
the world so flatly; the bay—a slice
of obsidian: blessed, iced, immovable.

FOUR PORTRAITS OF FIRE

1

I find a strange knowledge of wind,
an open door in the mountain
pass where everything intersects.
Believe me. This will not pass.
This is a world where flags
contain themselves, and are still,
marked by their unfurled edges.
Lean stuff sways on the boughs
of pitch pine: silver, almost tinsel,
all light gone blue and sprouting
orange oils in a last bouquet.

2

These were the nest builders;
I caught one last morning, I sang
so it fell down, stupid,
from the trees. They're so incorrect
in their dead skin. Witness their twig
feet, the mistake of their hands.
They will follow you. They yearn
pebbles for their gullets to grind
their own seed. They swallow
so selflessly and die
like patriots.

3

Last Christmas, a family of five
woke from their dreaming and
dreamed themselves over: the baby
in its pink pajamas, the boy
in the red flannel bathrobe
he grabbed from the door,
a mother, a father, and a sister
in curlers; all died.

A wood frame house,
a cannister of oil,
a match—watch
as it unsettles.
They were so cold;
umber.

4

I am away from the knowledge
of animal mystics,
brujas and sorcerers
or the nudging chants
of a Tlingit Kachina.
I am frightened by regions
with wills of their own,
but when my people
die in the snow
I wonder
did the depths billow up
to reach them?

STARFISH

They were lovely in the quartz and jasper sand
As if they had created terrariums with their bodies
On purpose; adding sprigs of seaweed, seashells,
White feathers, eel bones, miniature
Mussels, a fish jaw. Hundreds; no—
Thousands of baby stars. We touched them,
Surprised to find them soft, pliant, almost
Living in their attitudes. We would dry them, arrange them,
Form seascapes, geodesics . . . We gathered what we could
In the approaching darkness. Then we left hundreds of
Thousands of flawless five-fingered specimens sprawled
Along the beach as far as we could see, all massed
Together: little martyrs, soldiers, artless suicides
In lifelong liberation from the sea. So many
Splayed hands, the tide shoveled in.

IN JANUARY

That old man at the corner
keeps casting his rod.
What can he possibly snag
in this invisible season?
He reels it in.
He is all smile and bulging pockets.
His gray eyes are glazed
with the iridescence of his age.
His cheeks hold the last ash.
And though his daughter
is bringing him pillows and tea
and the handsome son-in-law
bends the line, a slow thing
stirs in the shadow of the bougainvillea.

SPIDERS

Above the calm exterior of roses, spiders bloom
fat with the afternoon buzzings.
They are harmless.
They are keeping the flies
off my back porch.
They have beautiful women
drawn on their bodies.
Their legs are ugly
but useful;
look what they leave
in the dew. Look.

FROM WHERE WE SIT: CORPUS CHRISTI

We watch seabirds flock the tour boat.
They feed from the tourist hand.

We who have learned the language
they speak as they beg

understand what they really say
as they lower and bite.

AN INTERPRETATION OF DINNER
BY THE UNINVITED GUEST

In the evening dusk when earth
is half star, half rock of red light,
when heaven opens to let out her crew
of white, bread-cheeked angels, marching
on to moral wars,
at six, exactly, the family
sits to supper. I watch them
in secret from my second floor apartment.
All hands, I see a Punch and Judy
farce: the right and left take turns.
The window is their stage. They perform
for me, alone. They pass. They set.
Their pats of butter, stewing
the tears from the fleshy buns;
and finally, they settle their places,
unfold their napkins, and begin
the feast.

I am alone and hungry
and I watch this every night
from my voting booth room.
If I turned on the light
they would see me. But I never.
The hands would reattach themselves
and who knows what country
their bodies dwell in.

POEM FOR THE YOUNG WHITE MAN
WHO ASKED ME HOW I, AN INTELLIGENT,
WELL-READ PERSON COULD BELIEVE
IN THE WAR BETWEEN RACES

In my land there are no distinctions.
The barbed wire politics of oppression
have been torn down long ago. The only reminder
of past battles, lost or won, is a slight
rutting in the fertile fields.

In my land
people write poems about love,
full of nothing but contented childlike syllables.
Everyone reads Russian short stories and weeps.
There are no boundaries.
There is no hunger, no
complicated famine or greed.

I am not a revolutionary.
I don't even like political poems.
Do you think I can believe in a war between races?
I can deny it. I can forget about it
when I'm safe,
living on my own continent of harmony
and home, but I am not
there.

I believe in revolution
because everywhere the crosses are burning,
sharp-shooting goose-steppers round every corner,
there are snipers in the schools . . .
(I know you don't believe this.
You think this is nothing
but faddish exaggeration. But they
are not shooting at you.)

I'm marked by the color of my skin.
The bullets are discrete and designed to kill slowly.
They are aiming at my children.
These are facts.
Let me show you my wounds: my stumbling mind, my
"excuse me" tongue, and this
nagging preoccupation
with the feeling of not being good enough.

These bullets bury deeper than logic.
Racism is not intellectual.
I can not reason these scars away.

Outside my door
there is a real enemy
who hates me.

I am a poet
who yearns to dance on rooftops,
to whisper delicate lines about joy
and the blessings of human understanding.
I try. I go to my land, my tower of words and
bolt the door, but the typewriter doesn't fade out
the sounds of blasting and muffled outrage.
My own days bring me slaps on the face.
Every day I am deluged with reminders
that this is not
my land

and this is my land.

I do not believe in the war between races

but in this country
there is war.

TO MY BROTHER

and for the lumpen bourgeoisie

We were so poor.
The air was a quiver
of thoughts we drew from

to poise, unsaid
in the ineffable
world we lived in.

Sun, scarcely a penny
in that dreary setting,
every night gave up

to a smog-strewn avalanche
of searchlights, crossing
the heavens, a bicker

to buy a new used car,
a four-door sedan, a six
month guarantee. I worked

the years through, thought
I could work my mind's way
out of there, out of needing

a dime bag of uppers for the next
buzzing shift. We paid our bills.
We were brilliant at wishing.

Our dreams wafted over the sullen skyline
like crazy meteors of flying embers:
a glow in the heart all night.

FREEWAY 280

Las casitas near the gray cannery,
nestled amid wild abrazos of climbing roses
and man-high red geraniums
are gone now. The freeway conceals it
all beneath a raised scar.

But under the fake windsounds of the open lanes,
in the abandoned lots below, new grasses sprout,
wild mustard remembers, old gardens
come back stronger than they were,
trees have been left standing in their yards.
Albaricoqueros, cerezos, nogales . . .
Viejitas come here with paper bags to gather greens.
Espinaca, verdolagas, yerbabuena . . .

I scramble over the wire fence
that would have kept me out.
Once, I wanted out, wanted the rigid lanes
to take me to a place without sun,
without the smell of tomatoes burning
on swing shift in the greasy summer air.

Maybe it's here
en los campos extraños de esta ciudad
where I'll find it, that part of me
mown under
like a corpse
or a loose seed.

BARCO DE REFUGIADOS

Como almidón de maíz
me deslizo, pasando por los ojos de mi abuela,
bíblia a su lado. Se quita los lentes.
El pudín se hace espeso.

Mamá me crío sin lenguaje.
Soy huérfano de mi nombre español.
Las palabras son extrañas,
tartamudeando en mi lengua.
Mis ojos ven el espejo, mi reflejo:
piel de bronce, cabello negro.

Siento que soy un cautivo
a bordo de un barco de refugiados.
El barco que nunca atraca.
El barco que nunca atraca.

REFUGEE SHIP

Like wet cornstarch, I slide
past my grandmother's eyes. Bible
at her side, she removes her glasses.
The pudding thickens.

Mama raised me without language.
I'm orphaned from my Spanish name.
The words are foreign, stumbling
on my tongue. I see in the mirror
my reflection: bronzed skin, black hair.

I feel I am a captive
aboard the refugee ship.
The ship that will never dock.
El barco que nunca atraca.

POEMA PARA LOS CALIFORNIOS MUERTOS

Once a refuge for Mexican Californios . . .
—plaque outside a restaurant
in Los Altos, California, 1974.

These older towns die
into stretches of freeway.
The high scaffolding cuts a clean cesarean
across belly valleys and fertile dust.
What a bastard child, this city
lost in the soft
llorando de las madres.
Californios moan like husbands of the raped,
husbands de la tierra,
tierra la madre.

I run my fingers
across this brass plaque.
Its cold stirs in me a memory
of silver buckles and spent bullets,
of embroidered shawls and dark rebozos.
Yo recuerdo los antepasados muertos.
Los recuerdo en la sangre,
la sangre fértil.

What refuge did you find here,
ancient Californios?
Now at this restaurant nothing remains
but this old oak and an ill-placed plaque.
Is it true that you still live here
in the shadows of these white, high-class houses?
Soy la hija pobrecita
pero puedo maldecir estas fantasmas blancas.
Las fantasmas tuyas deben aquí quedarse,
solas las tuyas.

In this place I see nothing but strangers.
On the shelves there are bitter antiques,
yanqui remnants
y estos no de los Californios.
A blue jay shrieks
above the pungent odor of crushed
eucalyptus and the pure scent
of rage.

OAXACA, 1974

México,
I look for you all day in the streets of Oaxaca.
The children run to me, laughing,
spinning me blind and silly.
They call to me in words of another language.
My brown body searches the streets
for the dye that will color my thoughts.

But México gags,
¡Esputa!
on this bland pochaseed.

I didn't ask to be brought up tonta!
My name hangs about me like a loose tooth.
Old women know my secret,
"Es la culpa de los antepasados."
Blame it on the old ones.
They give me a name
that fights me.

VISIONS OF MEXICO WHILE
AT A WRITING SYMPOSIUM
IN PORT TOWNSEND, WASHINGTON

México

When I'm that far south, the old words
molt off my skin, the feathers
of all my nervousness.
My own words somersault naturally as my name,
joyous among all those meadows: Michoacán,
Vera Cruz, Tenochtitlán, Oaxaca . . .
Pueblos green on the low hills
where men slap handballs below acres of maíz.
I watch and understand.
My frail body has never packed mud
or gathered in the full weight of the harvest.
Alone with the women in the adobe, I watch men,
their taut faces holding in all their youth.
This far south we are governed by the law
of the next whole meal. We work
and watch seabirds elbow their wings
in migratory ways, those mispronouncing gulls
coming south
to refuge or gameland.

I don't want to pretend I know more
and can speak all the names. I can't.
My sense of this land can only ripple through my veins
like the chant of an epic corrido.
I come from a long line of eloquent illiterates
whose history reveals what words don't say.
Our anger is our way of speaking,
the gesture is an utterance more pure than word.

We are not animals
but our senses are keen and our reflexes,
accurate punctuation.
All the knifings in a single night, low-voiced
scufflings, sirens, gunnings . . .
We hear them
and the poet within us bays.

Washington

I don't belong this far north.
The uncomfortable birds gawk at me.
They hem and haw from their borders in the sky.
I heard them say: México is a stumbling comedy.
A loose-legged Cantinflas woman
acting with Pancho Villa drunkenness.
Last night at the tavern
this was all confirmed
in a painting of a woman: her glowing
silk skin, a halo
extending from her golden coiffure
while around her, dark-skinned men with Jap slant eyes
were drooling in a caricature of machismo.
Below it, at the bar, two Chicanas
hung at their beers. They had painted black
birds that dipped beneath their eyelids.
They were still as foam while the men
fiddled with their asses, absently;
the bubbles of their teased hair snapped
open in the forced wind of the beating fan.

there are songs in my head I could sing you
songs that could drone away
all the Mariachi bands you thought you ever heard
songs that could tell you what I know
or have learned from my people
but for that   I need words
simple black nymphs between white sheets of paper
obedient words   obligatory words   words I steal
in the dark when no one can hear me

as pain sends seabirds south from the cold
I come north
to gather my feathers
for quills

iii

Emplumada

THIS MORNING

This morning stilled to a moment
of pure dreaming.

I looked out over the long grass
of winter light and rain, and saw

a hundred robins, as red in belly
as drunkards, all soaking it up,

telling it their way. They were there,
posing like boxers on the worming

earth. They were throwing their heads
behind them as the water rolled.

It was as if they were laughing, as if
the whole soaking world was something to laugh.

They were an element of song.
They had the ultimate authority

to do things. I watched them
through the greased window, watched

the living reduce to a bad reproduction
of streaks and misprints. Just when clarity

dings like a bell of sunlight, the blade
of grass, the vision, changes. The light

dives and I dream, incomprehensible
dreams of stars imploding, supernovas,

the black holes of sex. I dream all I could ever be,
all I would dare describe. I wake in sweat,

hear the roar of surf made by the swishing autos.
I wonder if I dare

get out of bed. My head, that heron's egg
sits on top of my shoulders, all bone and misleavings,

all drool and mumbling words. All signals
droning in my brain simmer to a whine

of silence so shrill
only a dog could hear.

I am driven from this world, alive.
I come to this world, in dreams.

CAFE SOLO

I loved you
with the scientific
excuse of the lonely.
Now I watch the streets
smog out of focus
or zoom in brutally
on the tragically beautiful.
My eyes have met no one's
all morning. I have forgotten
the purr of my name.
I remember only the brush
of my cat's teeth
when she tells me
she loves me. For weeks
the only lesson I've learned
is that the leaves of the apple
are finally turning. Everything
has let go. There are days now
that go by without a sound.
I could be anyone.
Once I was a person
who loved you.

BEETLES

A man who once loved me, told me
I knew nothing of beauty.
He had loved a double
more beautiful than I.

I'm hexed by a girl of pale heart,
a dove who wouldn't circle in day.
The thighs of her jeans are speckled with mustard.
Her hands are in her pockets too much of the time;
if they left, they would be birds, fragile, humming.
They are right where she puts them.
She's a farmer, plowing
the gray dirt.
She loves the land, its
ugliness.

I'm an ugly woman, weedlike,
elbowing my way through the perfect
grass. The best of what I am
is in the gravel behind the train yard
where obsidian chips lodge
in the rocks like beetles.
I burrow and glow.

FOR ALL YOU KNOW

I could call myself Lilith,
or Edith or Ed. I would not change
the way I look to you. You know me
too well. You know me not at all.
I've stories to tell you: my religion,
for instance, I've spoken to God
but he was a flock of crows, and who
would believe it? I have an aunt
who murdered her husband in bed,
drew a target in lipstick, then
punctured the bull's-eye with methodical
whimsy. My mother gave birth
to a blue doll struck dumb
from the start. I've seen whales
leaping, rattlers give up the ghost.
For all you know, I've given up
writing lies that could suck you
into orgasms of small mercies.
For all you know,
I could be simple,
cook a fine meal,
hike without sweating,
carve Christ figures in secret.
For all you know,
I could let you cry out in front of me.
I wouldn't say a word
and say everything.

COMO LO SIENTO

I heard an owl at midday.
A crow flew, spiraled, drifted,
and I thought of the circle
my own life made, and how
at heart I'm a hoverer
the way I've always drifted
toward you.
Another owl lifted from the palm.
She showed me how I rose, caught
in the wind by your skin and tongue.
I feel scooped from the banks like clay,
smoked and fired by your eyes
til I ring. I'm paralyzed by joy
and I forget how to act.
I'm a shell in the cliffs.
a thousand miles from sea.
You tide me and I rise,
and there's no truth
more simple.

THE BODY AS BRAILLE

He tells me, "Your back
is so beautiful." He traces
my spine with his hand.

I'm burning like the white ring
around the moon. "A witch's moon,"
dijo mi abuela. The schools call it

"a reflection of ice crystals."
It's a storm brewing in the cauldron
of the sky. I'm in love

but won't tell him
if it's omens
or ice.

MOONWALKERS

In rarefied air, absent as lovers,
Objects are blanched and peppered to gray,

Flushed belly-up, sincerely
Drawn by their weightlessness;

We are not alone this night, walking,
Searching for a distinguisher

Between the bare witness of moon,
Love, we are together in this: for good.

SHELLS

I string shells
put an order
to my life

I find in shells
the way I live
everything I touch

is fragile
but full of color
or brine

I can't
hold back
from touching

§

stranger
not my husband
you offer

seabirds
cleft surf
the sun

ripping apart
the fog-strewn
shoreline

§

I am young
balloon-mad
the child in me

scatters down the coast
off the pebbled beach
of Point Reyes

that was another time
I bordered my pale life
with the colors

of hallucinogens
every pebble
was a wonder

I could name
only by color
jade   vermilion

sandstone   buff
or the inexplicable
azure glass

I was alone
gathering
the polished stones

I still hold
dear—for me now
every joy

measures itself
against the brilliance
of that time

§

you said
you suffered
a sheltered life

I want to scratch
that envy
from your voice

I take refuge
in the fact
that every

pleasure
I've worked myself
like the fireplace

my grandmother built
still standing
all these years

every stone
set furiously
in place

§

I dust pebbles
turn them
to sheen

what I want
is an unnamed
thing

when you have gone
I wonder at the way
I let you go

without touching
you, wonder
at seagulls, the

danger in their willful
lines—for them
life is nothing

but picking
the coast clean
all they love

is a flicker of bread
or the opening
of another hand

BEFORE YOU GO

Remember this twist:
remember how the charcoal
found its way out of your hand,
how the lives feel under
your power. You were a world
gone inside out. When I touched you
there was coal on my pillow all night.

What little hope we had
is not ours yet. The fence
to the frozen yard is duned
in snow. Something speaks to us both
in a cloud of geese. They hum
as they go. They have yet
to reach song. Dear,

I was a girl. I was juniper
or magnolia, all violet and rage.
Marmots, foxfire, black
rememberings in the scrub, now
I remember our rusted buckets
as we gathered sour apples
in the winds, your long hair,
matting to silver and gold,
the shimmer of your teared eyes
gone cold.

FOR JOHN ON THE CAPE

Your sun shone on the headlands,
glass matched on the little beams
like the phosphorescence of a hawk's
gold eye. It was like seeing you
for the first time: our time was mooning
away from us and leaving us in mudflats.
Understand. This was hope of a kind,
a bare, prenatal longing and return.

Because we will never be serious
we have come to these shores —
alive, in love, and teeming.

Together, waist-high in the lapping
penumbra of hours, we stall,
and are left wondering

where we ever found
such loyalty.

ORANGES

An old woman passed, crossing herself,
her eyes burning winter oranges.
I felt the painting Grandma hung in her
room: two children holding, reinlike,
the fraying rope of a broken bridge.
The black storm and lightning flash
illuminated the dead fish below,
                      and beside them,
their Guardian Angel, unnoticed as air,
her arms, a net to break their fall.
I believed it would be.
Her breath held me that instant.
The air frays to sheen
and we are guided out
of falling.

EMPLUMADA

When summer ended
the leaves of snapdragons withered
taking their shrill-colored mouths with them.
They were still, so quiet. They were
violet where umber now is. She hated
and she hated to see
them go. Flowers

born when the weather was good—this
she thinks of, watching the branch of peaches
daring their ways above the fence, and further,
two hummingbirds, hovering, stuck to each other,
arcing their bodies in grim determination
to find what is good, what is
given them to find. These are warriors

distancing themselves from history.
They find peace
in the way they contain the wind
and are gone.

GLOSSARY OF SPANISH
WORDS AND PHRASES

I

"Meeting Mescalito at Oak Hill Cemetery"
  Mescalito—a spirit inhabiting the peyote cactus

"Beneath the Shadow of the Freeway"
  Los Altos—the heights
  Sal Si Puedes—get out if you can; a barrio (neighborhood) in East San
    José, California
  borrachando—on a binge (*borracho*—a drunk)

"Caribou Girl"
  con un abrazo—with an embrace

II

"Freeway 280"
  Las casitas—the little houses
  abrazos—bear hugs
  Albaricoqueros . . . —apricot trees, cherry trees, walnut trees
  Viejitas—old women (*-itas*—diminutive connoting affection)
  Espinaca . . . —spinach, purslane, mint
  en los campos . . . —in the strange fields of this city

"Poema Para los Californios Muertos"
  Poema . . . —poem for the dead Californios (*Californios*—original
    inhabitants when California was still Mexico)
  llorando de las madres—crying of the mothers
  de la tierra . . . —of the land, the mother earth
  Yo recuerdo . . .—I remember the dead ancestors. I remember them in
    my blood, my fertile blood.
  Soy tu hija . . . —I am only your poor daughter, but I can curse these
    white ghosts. Only your ghosts should remain here, only yours.

"Oaxaca, 1974"
  Esputa/Es puta—is a whore (*escupa*—spit)
  pochaseed/pocha—an assimilated Mexican American
  tonta—stupid, foolish; a dolt
  Es la culpa . . . —It's her ancestors' fault.

"Visions of Mexico . . ."
  maíz—corn
  corrido—an epic Mexican ballad
  Cantinflas—a Mexican comedian similar to Charlie Chaplin
  machismo—masculinity; macho

III

"Como lo Siento"
  Como lo siento—how I feel (about it)

"The Body as Braille"
  dijo mi abuela—my grandmother told me

PITT POETRY SERIES
Ed Ochester, General Editor

Dannie Abse, *Collected Poems*
Adonis, *The Blood of Adonis*
Jack Anderson, *Toward the Liberation of the Left Hand*
Jon Anderson, *Death & Friends*
Jon Anderson, *In Sepia*
Jon Anderson, *Looking for Jonathan*
John Balaban, *After Our War*
Gerald W. Barrax, *Another Kind of Rain*
Michael Benedikt, *The Badminton at Great Barrington; Or, Gustave Mahler
  & the Chattanooga Choo-Choo*
Lorna Dee Cervantes, *Emplumada*
Robert Coles, *A Festering Sweetness: Poems of American People*
Leo Connellan, *First Selected Poems*
Fazıl Hüsnü Dağlarca, *Selected Poems*
Norman Dubie, *Alehouse Sonnets*
Norman Dubie, *In the Dead of the Night*
Stuart Dybek, *Brass Knuckles*
Odysseus Elytis, *The Axion Esti*
John Engels, *Blood Mountain*
John Engels, *Signals from the Safety Coffin*
Brendan Galvin, *The Minutes No One Owns*
Brendan Galvin, *No Time for Good Reasons*
Gary Gildner, *Digging for Indians*
Gary Gildner, *First Practice*
Gary Gildner, *Nails*
Gary Gildner, *The Runner*
Mark Halperin, *Backroads*
Patricia Hampl, *Woman Before an Aquarium*
Michael S. Harper, *Song: I Want a Witness*
John Hart, *The Climbers*
Samuel Hazo, *Blood Rights*
Samuel Hazo, *Once for the Last Bandit: New and Previous Poems*
Samuel Hazo, *Quartered*
Gwen Head, *Special Effects*
Gwen Head, *The Ten Thousandth Night*
Milne Holton and Graham W. Reid, eds., *Reading the Ashes: An Anthology of
  the Poetry of Modern Macedonia*
Milne Holton and Paul Vangelisti, eds., *The New Polish Poetry: A Bilingual
  Collection*
David Huddle, *Paper Boy*

Shirley Kaufman, *The Floor Keeps Turning*
Shirley Kaufman, *From One Life to Another*
Shirley Kaufman, *Gold Country*
Ted Kooser, *Sure Signs: New and Selected Poems*
Abba Kovner, *A Canopy in the Desert: Selected Poems*
Paul-Marie Lapointe, *The Terror of the Snows: Selected Poems*
Larry Levis, *Wrecking Crew*
Jim Lindsey, *In Lieu of Mecca*
Tom Lowenstein, tr., *Eskimo Poems from Canada and Greenland*
Archibald MacLeish, *The Great American Fourth of July Parade*
Peter Meinke, *The Night Train and The Golden Bird*
Peter Meinke, *Trying to Surprise God*
Judith Minty, *In the Presence of Mothers*
James Moore, *The New Body*
Carol Muske, *Camouflage*
Leonard Nathan, *Dear Blood*
Sharon Olds, *Satan Says*
Gregory Pape, *Border Crossings*
Thomas Rabbitt, *Exile*
Ed Roberson, *Etai-Eken*
Ed Roberson, *When Thy King Is A Boy*
Eugene Ruggles, *The Lifeguard in the Snow*
Dennis Scott, *Uncle Time*
Herbert Scott, *Groceries*
Richard Shelton, *The Bus to Veracruz*
Richard Shelton, *Of All the Dirty Words*
Richard Shelton, *You Can't Have Everything*
Gary Soto, *The Elements of San Joaquin*
Gary Soto, *The Tale of Sunlight*
David Steingass, *American Handbook*
Tomas Tranströmer, *Windows & Stones: Selected Poems*
Alberta T. Turner, *Learning to Count*
Alberta T. Turner, *Lid and Spoon*
Chase Twichell, *Northern Spy*
Constance Urdang, *The Lone Woman and Others*
Cary Waterman, *The Salamander Migration and Other Poems*
Bruce Weigl, *A Romance*
David P. Young, *The Names of a Hare in English*
David P. Young, *Sweating Out the Winter*